D1163637

U.S. Army

BY LINDA BOZZO

amicus
high interest

Amicus High Interest is an imprint of Amicus
P.O. Box 1329, Mankato, MN 56002
www.amicuspublishing.us

Library of Congress Cataloging-in-Publication Data
Bozzo, Linda.
 U.S. Army / by Linda Bozzo.
    p. cm. — (Serving in the military)
 Includes index.
 Audience: Grades K-3.
 Summary: "An introduction to what the US Army is, what
recruits do, and jobs soldiers could learn. Includes descriptions
of missions to save the Baghdad Zoo and give aid to the 2011
Gulf of Mexico oil spill"—Provided by publisher.
 ISBN 978-1-60753-389-4 (library binding)
 ISBN 978-1-60753-437-2 (ebook)
 1. United States. Army—Juvenile literature. I. Title.
 UA25.B62 2014
 355.00973—dc23

                               2012036228

Editor   Wendy Dieker
Designer Kathleen Petelinsek

Photo Credits: Corbis/Rob Howard cover; Corbis/Bettmann
26; Corbis/Peter Beck 14; Corbis/Reuters 9; Corbis/Sgt. Sean
Patrick Casey/US Army/Handout/Digital 22; Corbis/Staff Sgt.
Tate Petersen/US Army/Handout/Digital 20-21; Dreamstime/
Robert Scholl 18; Getty Images/Arthur Meyerson 24-25; Getty
Images/Jacom Stephens 10; Getty Images/Joe Raedle 6; Getty
Images/Ro-Ma Stock Photography 16-17; Getty Images/Skip
Brown 13; US Department of Defense/Spc. Charles W. Gill 4;
US Department of Defense/Tech. Sgt. James Mossman, U.S. Air
Force 29

Printed in the United States at Corporate Graphics in
North Manakato, Minnesota
4-2013 / 1150
10 9 8 7 6 5 4 3 2 1

Table of Contents

Saving the Zoo

It is 2003. The United States has attacked the city of Baghdad in Iraq. Caught in the middle of the fight is a large zoo. **Mortar shells** and gunfire leave holes everywhere. The zoo is home to over 600 animals. But now it is destroyed. The zoo workers have left for safety.

An army soldier guards the gate at the Baghdad Zoo.

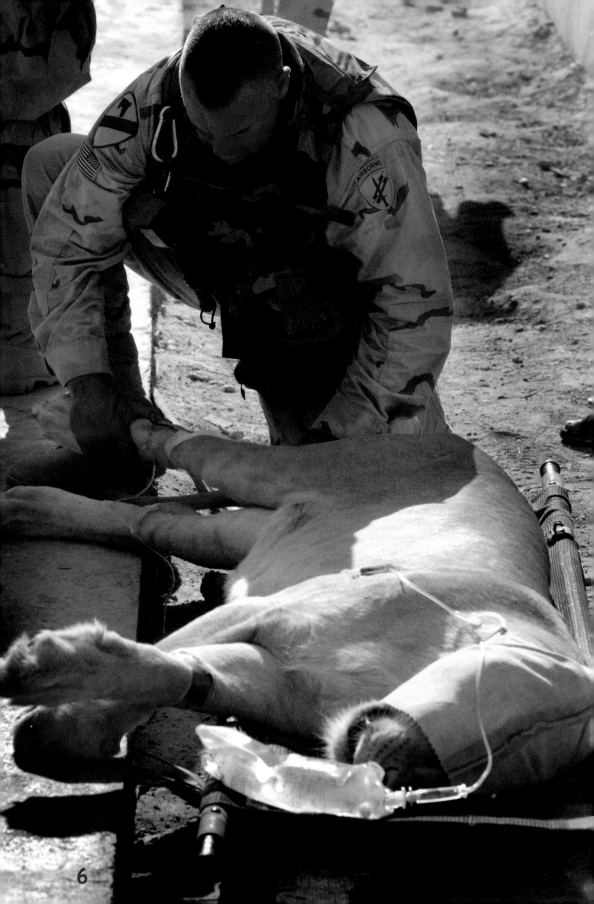

A team of soldiers is called in. They have a special job. Many of the animals are missing. Cages are ruined. Lions and tigers are loose in the streets. Many of the animals do not have food or water. They have no place to live. Supplies used to run the zoo are gone. Help is needed fast!

A soldier helps move a lion to a safe place.

A team of soldiers, **veterinarians**, and **volunteers** begin to work. They make repairs. They bring in food and supplies. Sick animals are helped. Soldiers search for missing animals. After lots of work, the zoo is finally reopened. The animals are safe. The mission is a success!

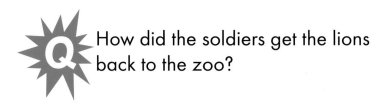

How did the soldiers get the lions back to the zoo?

A bear is brought back to the zoo.

 Soldiers found the lions. They brought them back to the zoo in armored fighting trucks.

A team of soldiers watches for danger. They are ready!

 How many soldiers are in the U.S. Army?

Learning the Ropes

The U.S. Army is one big team. They work to keep our country safe. Soldiers fight on the ground in big tanks. They fly in helicopters and jets. Ever wonder what it takes to be a soldier? It takes hard work. But the first step is learning the ropes.

 Lots! There are about 480,000 full time soldiers in the U.S. Army.

New members of the army are called **recruits**. They must finish ten weeks of basic training. They train to be strong and fit. Skills like marching and drills are taught. They learn to use **weapons**. At the end of basic training, it is time to graduate!

 What types of drills do recruits perform?

Soldiers learn to march in step. It takes practice!

 They practice standing at attention. They practice saluting. There are even rest positions.

Soldiers are now ready for advanced training. This is where they learn skills to do their job. There are over 100 army jobs to do. Some people train as officers. They will lead a team of soldiers. Most train for jobs on the field. Some will work in offices.

Jobs in offices are important. These soldiers send messages.

Would you like to drive a military tank? Fly a helicopter? Your job could be to take care of weapons like rocket launchers or machine guns. A **paratrooper** jumps out of planes. Truck drivers are needed too. If you like to fix things you could be a **mechanic**. These are just a few army jobs.

Paratroopers learn to jump from planes.

The Home Front

On the home front soldiers work and train on a military base. Most of them live there too. Their main job is to train to fight. There are other jobs too. Truck drivers deliver supplies. Construction workers build new **barracks**, homes for soldiers. Men and women work in offices on computers.

Soldiers wear lots of gear when they practice fighting.

When trouble hits, the U.S. Army is called. Flood! Soldiers are called to clean up after disasters. Fire! Soldiers in Black Hawk helicopters fight wildfires. Another job is helping to keep peace during riots. They work to keep us safe. That is their job.

The army fights wildfires from above.

Soldiers work in the mountains of Afghanistan.

 How many U.S. military bases are there overseas?

Stationed Overseas

A job with the army could take you anywhere in the world. Army bases in other countries are important. They give aid to soldiers who are fighting. Machines break. Tanks and trucks need to get fixed. Supplies like food, clothing, and **ammunition** need to be stored. These bases let soldiers get to where the trouble is fast!

Around 900. The U.S. Army has bases in 130 countries.

Soldiers working overseas may find themselves closer to fights. Some drive tanks. Others keep weapons working. Enemies must be found and captured. Paratroopers jump by parachute out of planes. Officers are the leaders of the army. Everyone works together. They keep the skies and battlefields safe from enemies.

Tanks can drive on any kind of land.

Soldiers overseas must be prepared for anything. Enemies can attack at any time. Bombs can blow up. Disasters strike when least expected. A soldier's job is to protect our country's freedom. It is important to help keep peace around the world. The U.S. Army must be ready at all times.

Army soldiers use flamethrowers. Enemies better watch out!

Our Heroes

In May 2011, an **oil-drilling rig** blew up. Oil was leaking into the Gulf of Mexico. The U.S. Army used a floating bridge to carry supplies. These supplies helped to keep the oil from spreading.

The U.S. Army does jobs like this and more every day. Men and women who serve in the military are true heroes.

 Do soldiers receive rewards for their bravery?

Soldiers use a floating bridge to carry tanks across water.

 **A** Yes, soldiers receive the Medal of Honor for their bravery. It is a five-pointed star that hangs from a ribbon.

Glossary

ammunition Bullets fired from guns or bombs used in fighting wars.

barracks Buildings where soldiers live.

mechanic A person who fixes machines such as cars, trucks, or planes.

mortar shells The shells that are shot out of short cannons called mortars.

oil-drilling rig A machine that drills underwater to find oil and pump it to the surface.

paratrooper A soldier who is trained to jump from a plane with a parachute.

recruit A person who has just joined the military.

veterinarian A doctor for animals.

volunteers People who give their time or services free of charge.

weapon Something that a soldier uses to fight with, such as guns and bombs.

Read More

Bergin, Mark. *Soldiers. How to Draw.* New York: PowerKids Press, 2012.

Goldish, Meish. *Army: Civilian to Soldier. Becoming a Soldier.* New York: Bearport Publishing, 2011.

Markovics, Joyce L. *Today's Army Heroes. Acts of Courage: Inside America's Military.* New York: Bearport Publishing, 2012.

Websites

Brain Pop: Armed Forces
http://www.brainpop.com/socialstudies/ usgovernmentandlaw/armedforces/preview.weml

Enchanted Learning: Memorial Day
http://www.enchantedlearning.com/crafts/memorialday

United States Dept of Veteran Affairs
http://www.va.gov/kids/K-5/

Index

About the Author

Linda Bozzo is the author of more than 30 books for the school and library market. She would like to thank all of the men and women in the military for their outstanding service to our country. Visit her website at www.lindabozzo.com.